Film Actresses

Volume 17

Janet Gaynor

Documentary study

Part 1

ISBN-13 : 978-1502949141

ISBN-10 : 1502949148

Dtp
and
graphic design

Iacob Adrian

Author statement

The actors and actresses are the the bricks .

The cast and crew are the plaster .

They stand on the foundation created by
producers and writers and directors .

All these people creates the great palace
of the art of film .

Iacob Adrian - 2013

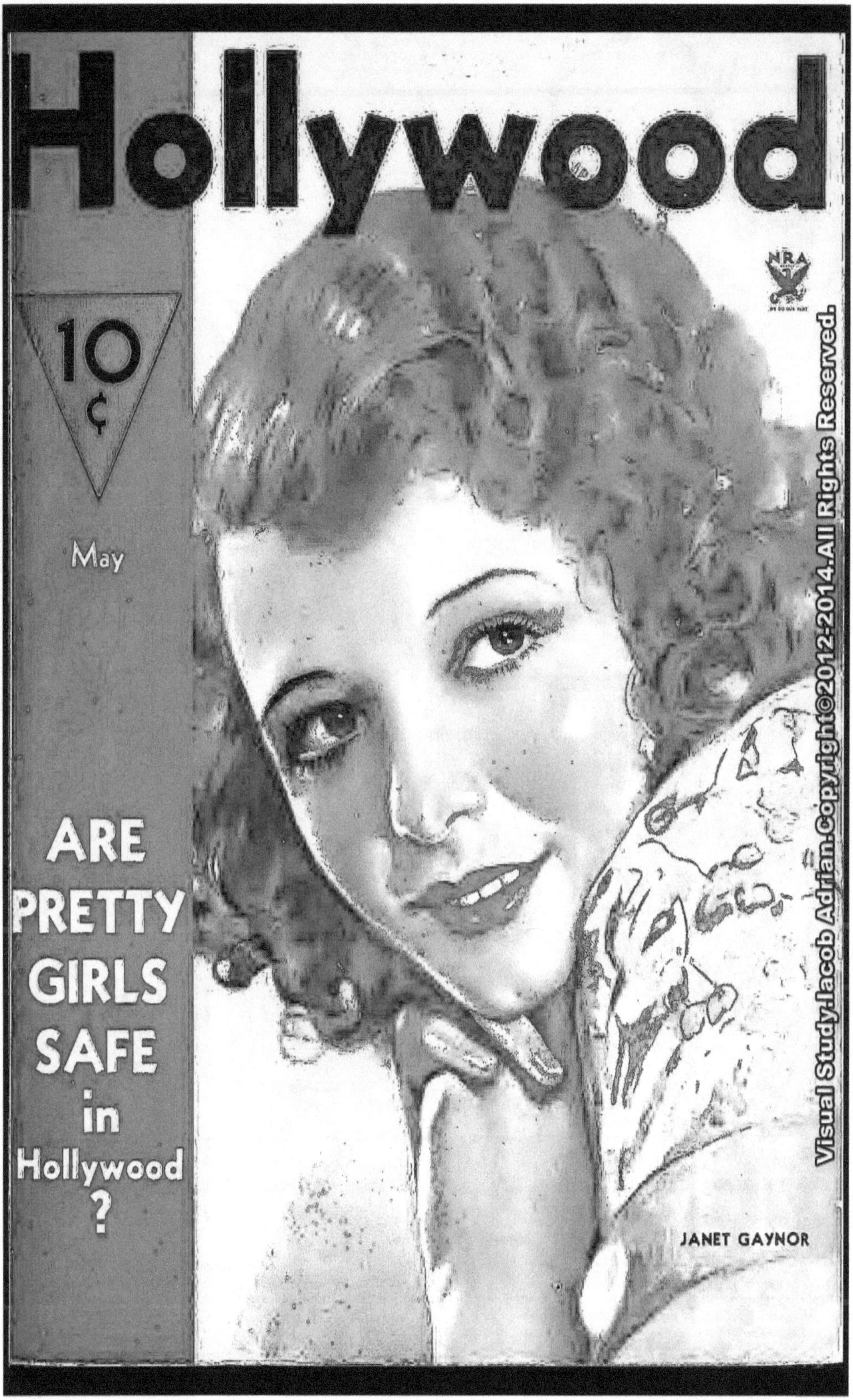

Hollywood

10¢

May

ARE
PRETTY
GIRLS
SAFE
in
Hollywood
?

JANET GAYNOR

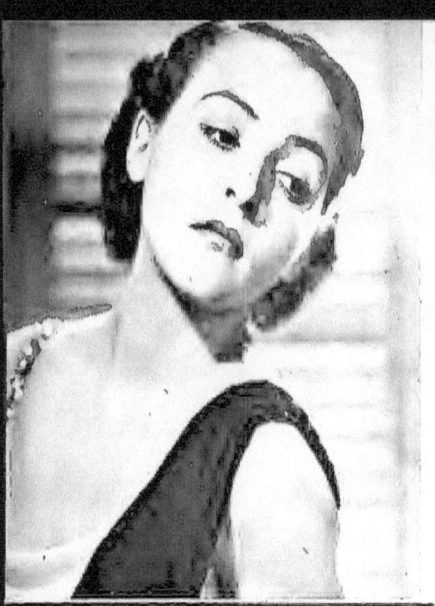

ADA CAVELL

—*Ernest A. Bachrach*

* Meet a young lady who is expected to contribute an important page to cinema history! Ada is scoring in *Crime Doctor*

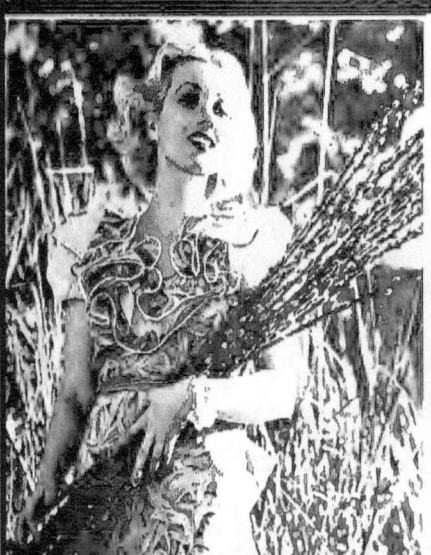

ANN SOTHERN

—*Orville Suider*

* Another sensational new "find," Ann (whose real name is Harriet Lake) excited raves by her work in Columbia's *Let's Fall in Love*. She was starred on Broadway in *Of Thee I Sing*

JANET GAYNOR

—*Otto Dyar*

* *The Sun Shines Bright* on Janet and all her fans for in the picture of this title she will again be teamed with Charles Farrell. She recently completed *Carolina*, which also offers Lionel Barrymore

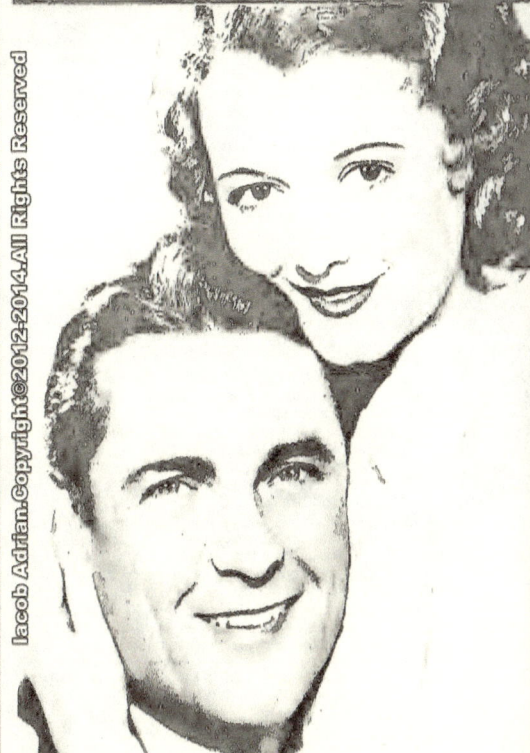

Together again

The most *Glorious*
sweethearts of the Screen

Janet
GAYNOR

Charles
FARRELL

Just as they captured your hearts in
"Seventh Heaven" and "Sunny Side Up",
they'll win you again in this lovable
romance of young hearts, young love—

CHANGE OF HEART

with
JAMES DUNN
GINGER ROGERS

Produced by WINFIELD SHEEHAN
Directed by John C. Blystone. From
the novel "Manhattan Love Song"
by Kathleen Norris

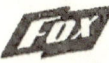

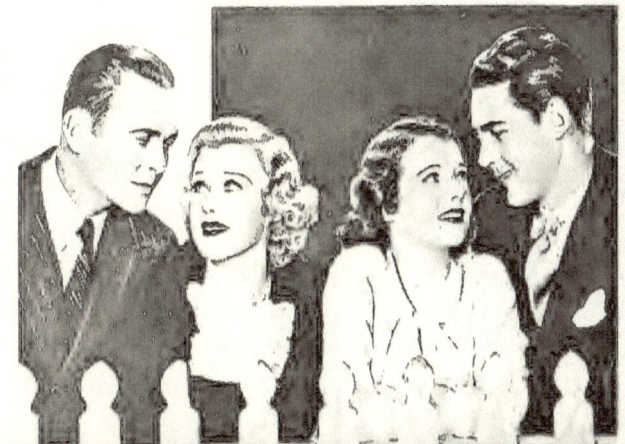

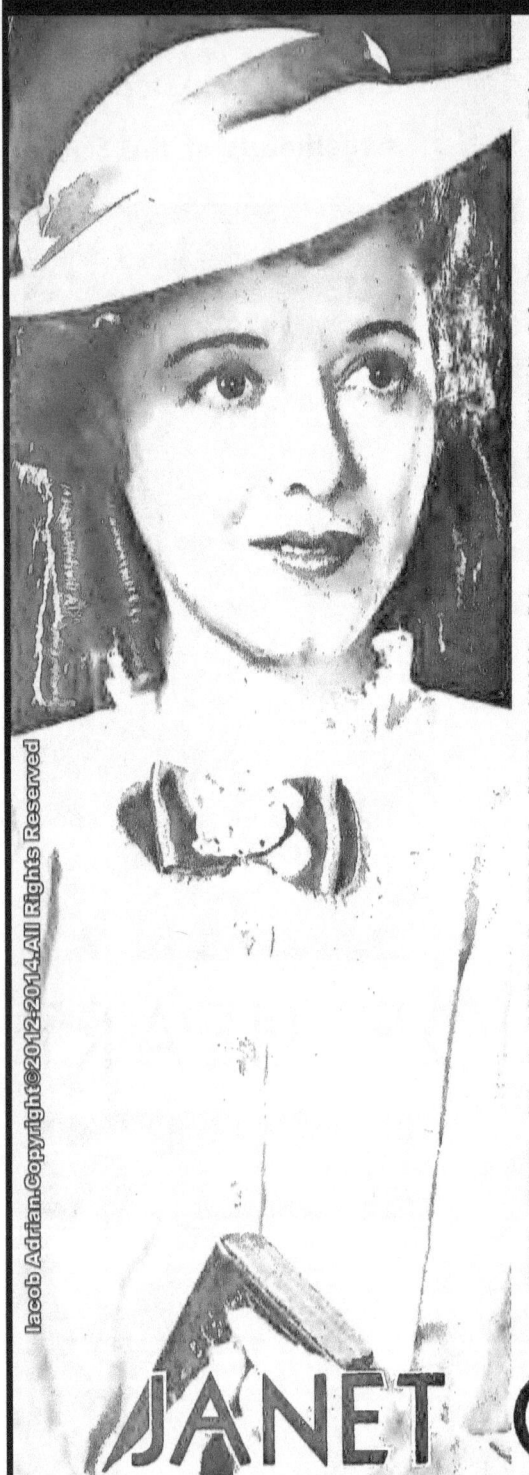

Janet Gaynor declares war on loneliness and un-happiness . . . and you'll be surprised at the result!

A NEW JANET GAYNOR is ready to face the world which she has shunned for over a year! Soon Hollywood will recognize her as the grown woman, no longer afraid of life, that she has become. The transformation is complete.

Idol of all small towns, butt of cruel Hollywood ridicule, Janet has been living an unheralded and unpublicized life such as Garbo could only imagine in her dreams.

It has been a strange picture—that of a girl whose fan mail and weekly salary check rank with any of the movie industry's most popular entertainers separated from her fellow workers by as wide a gulf as could come between people in the same business.

"What?" Janet exclaims. "Live among all those picture people and their petty squabbles? I should say not!"

● Janet doesn't forget that she is a picture person herself. She just can't convince herself that she is part and parcel of Hollywood. And she isn't! She works at the studio, draws her salary from a producer, and there the likeness ends.

She realized this when she withdrew from Hollywood society a year ago this spring and surrounded her private affairs with an inpenetrable cloak of silence.

But today she wants to try again. She wants to live, free and unhampered by her fear of what Hollywood might have to say. The heartbreak and discouragement which drove her into seclusion are things of the past. She has recovered her sense of equilibrium.

When Janet and Lydell Peck were divorced, Janet thought she wanted seclusion from everything Hollywood was. She broke all her ties with the cinema capital and plunged into an entirely new life, completely foreign to anything in the past.

At the time of her divorce, the harsh light of unfavorable criticism was being played on her work in pictures by sophisticated critics and snobbish actors. Rumors were abroad that Charles Farrell was largely responsible for the dissolution of her marriage ties. Sickened, Janet made up her mind to completely alienate herself from Hollywood.

Now the first keen hurt has been dulled. She wants to mingle again with those she tried to forget, live what she thinks would be a normal life for an actress. She decided to strike a happy compromise and it turned out to be the solution she was seeking. Yet she spurns the offers of a gay Hollywood whose only demand is that she become an integral part of it. That she will never do!

● Her life of the past few months has taught Janet that she must retain more of her individuality than do most of Hollywood's film stars, if she is to return to their life and be happy.

Three servants, a cook, a personal maid, and a chauffeur, run her home which stands between Beverly Hills and Hollywood. She lives here because she found it imperative to be in such close touch with her studio. Otherwise, her home would be miles from the capital of filmland.

She does manage to have her personal refuge to which she flees when it is vacation time. Malibu Beach is the natural choice of nearly every Hollywood personage of importance enough to afford its beach houses. Because Janet was only too well aware of this fact, she selected an

JANET GAYNOR

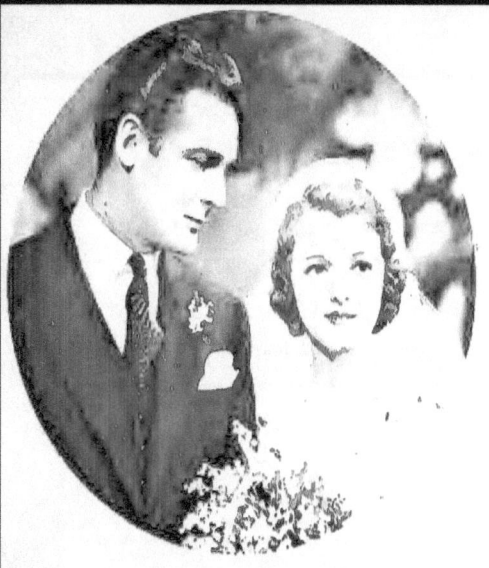

by FRED RUTLEDGE

Janet Gaynor is far too sensible to cherish dreams of a real-life wedding with Charles Farrell for she knows that while that is not impossible it is highly improbable

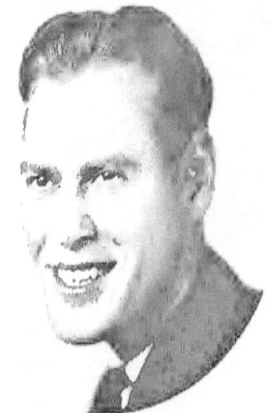

Following her divorce from Lydell Peck a year ago, Janet Gaynor became Hollywood's loneliest, most unhappy star

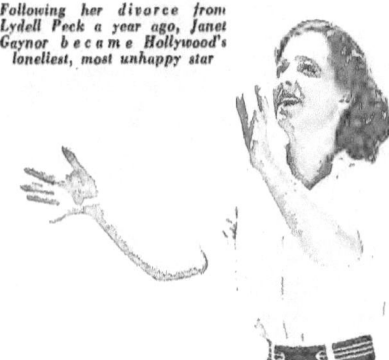

entirely different location for her own seaside bungalow.

It stands down at an unfashionable beach just past the oil wells at Venice, silent and nearly without neighbors. White sand stretches out in both directions, washed by the Pacific ocean. And there Janet stays, lying for long hours on a beach which has no other occupant.

Occasionally her closest neighbors are at home. They are Fay Wray and her husband, John Monk Saunders. Perhaps Janet will meet them on the sidewalk which runs along in front of their two cottages.

"Hello," Janet salutes them, and with a wave of her hand she is gone. Never another word, except a congratulation or two if a picture has just been released.

Back for work at her Beverly Hills home, Janet rests after studio hours in the cloistered privacy of a huge flower garden. She walks among the different beds, noticing with pleasure the artful effects they obtain, putting in the back of her head suggestions for slight changes she will make to the gardener.

The hardest part of living a life withdrawn from the community to which she owes her earnings has been the absence of enough spontaneous gaiety.

She has found that privacy, freedom from prying gentlemen of the press, rest from a constant round of parties, grow into almost insurmountable obstacles in a path to normal enjoyment of life.

It is all well and good to go two or three nights a week to the neighboring picture house without fanfare of studio publicity, to see a favorite star. It would be more than enough—if it were possible to stop and chat with people who were friends.

At first, in her seclusion, Janet cast around for obvious

Janet's beach home is segregated from those of other film stars. She has consistently avoided their companionship but now all that is over. She is resolved to forget the past and live only for today!

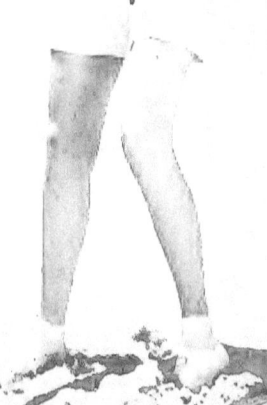

REBELS!

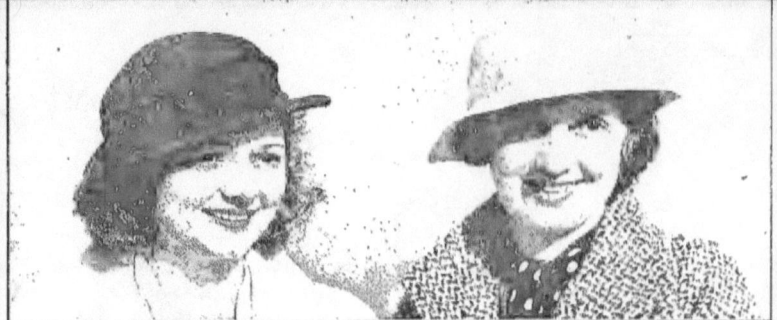

Janet Gaynor and her mother, Mrs. Laura Gaynor, are constant companions. Mrs. Gaynor has become a sister and confidante to her famous daughter and has helped immeasurably to ease the loneliness of Janet's solitary conquest of Hollywood

Janet Gaynor Rebels!

ways out of her dilemma, but the answers she found to her problem were temporary, too fleeting.

She entertained. Friends came to dinner or for weekends, but they were not Hollywood people, motion picture stars. They were usually from out of town.

She has tried traveling. Once, on her vacation wanderings, she found the Hawaiian Islands. Since that time she has made over a dozen trips to this paradise spot in the Pacific. It is one of her real delights to sing an island melody or dance in native rhythm for her small audiences.

However the Hawaiian Islands are not home. The natives are not her neighbors, her house guests. The time between visits, partially filled with work, still leaves enough space for days of solitude unbroken by the call from a single visitor.

Trips to New York have become frequent. With her mother, Janet starts out by train with only the briefest advance notice in the papers and her own studio publicity releases.

Her last visit to the Eastern metropolis affords a graphic picture of Janet's relations with the movie colony of Hollywood.

Just after her arrival she met an old friend. "Did you know that Mary Pickford is in town?" she was asked.

"Oh, is she?" Janet said absently. Then she smiled wistfully. "You know, I don't know her. I've only met her once or twice and that was just to say 'how do you do.' I know that she's very nice, though."

A motion picture star and not an acquaintance of Mary Pickford, the first lady in the social swirl of Hollywood! It seems almost incredible.

It has been written many times about Janet that Hollywood is unable to understand her, that she is in Hollywood but not of it. That is a picture of the old Janet. The new actress Hollywood will be able to recognize.

One of Janet's first steps towards her goal was taken last fall while she was on the set at the studio making *Paddy, The Next Best Thing*. Here she met her best friend, Margaret Lindsay.

It was the first time in many months Janet had found a girl she liked and respected who was a Hollywood actress. Their tastes parallel closely. It was the

beginning of Janet's growing belief that perhaps Hollywood people can appreciate her naturalness.

"If people in Hollywood only knew her as I do," Margaret says in support of Janet's theory, "how they would love her!"

There is one other person who has helped to fill Janet's long days — her mother. Because she is young looking, vivacious, and likes a good time, Laura Gaynor has become a sister, a confidante, an inseparable companion to her daughter. She has had no difficulty in understanding Janet's success in films.

Janet has used a great deal of her spare time studying. Dancing, voice culture, dramatics. It has been hard work, a long pull, but it has gone hand in hand with the growth of the new Janet. Now it is up to casting directors to grasp the fact that they have a glamorous, dramatic actress instead of the wistful, best-girl-friend Gaynor of the past.

She has slowly awakened to the realization that glamour, the precious halo which surrounds its owner with fame and respect, must be wooed to be won. So she is beginning to return to a small part of the night life that was hers when she was married.

It has become the favorite item of talk, when conversation glanced off onto Janet, to mention Charlie Farrell in the same breath.

No article about Janet has been complete without a discussion of this romantic interest. And almost to a man, they have all agreed that ultimate marriage was inevitable.

It is true that Janet will listen for long hours in rapt attention when Charles Farrell is the object of conversation. But he is married! Janet's good sense of proportion cannot help but take that into consideration.

A romance between these two, an unuttered dream of thousands of movie fans, is not impossible. But it is utterly improbable. How foolish it would be for Janet to waste her entire youth waiting, probably in vain!

And that is the secret of the new Janet. She has determined to stop wasting the short precious hours of her twenties. She is tired of traveling her road alone!

Janet Gaynor IN SERVANTS' ENTRANCE

ADVANCE VIEWS OF HER NEW PICTURE

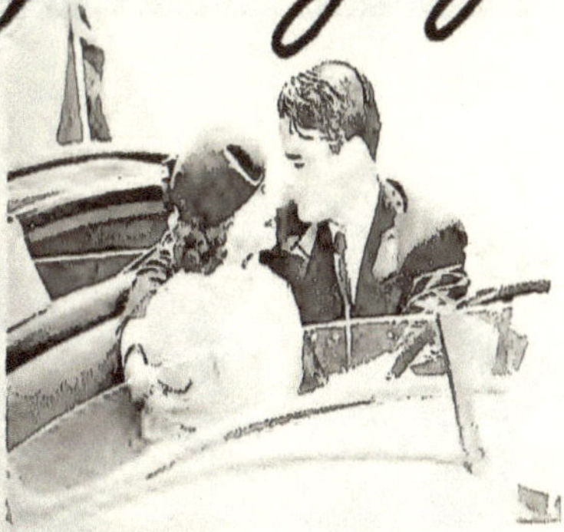

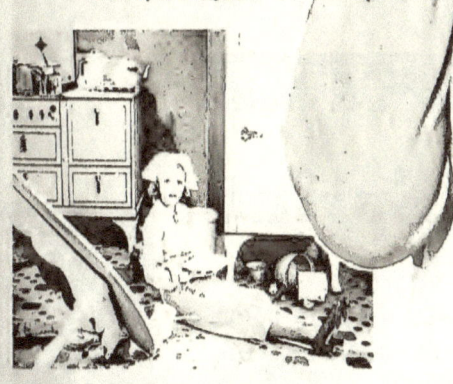

Love in a motorboat. The little rich girl learning to be poor (Janet) out for a spin with her employer's chauffeur (Lew Ayres)

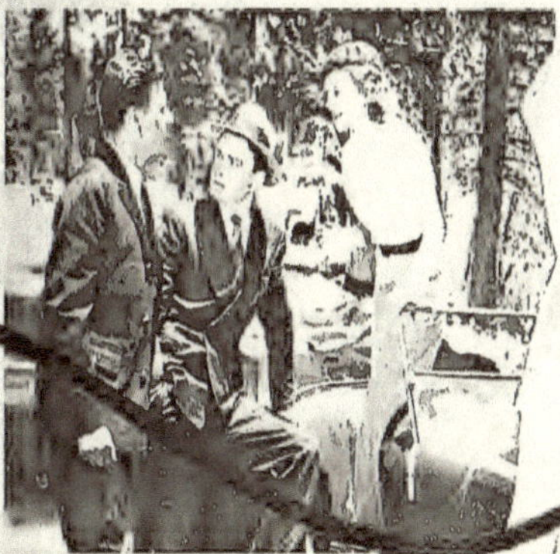

G. P. Huntley, Jr., who carved a name for himself in Little Man, What Now?; Lew Ayres and Janet

The kitchen may be a wreck, but thank heaven the pie's safe. Janet appears to be a little surprised about it all

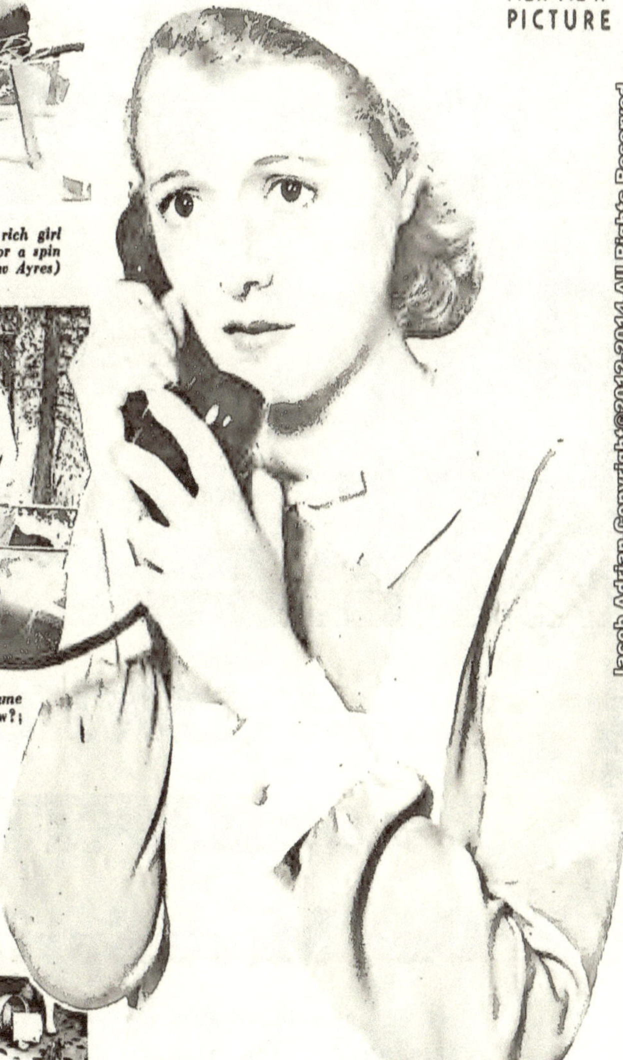

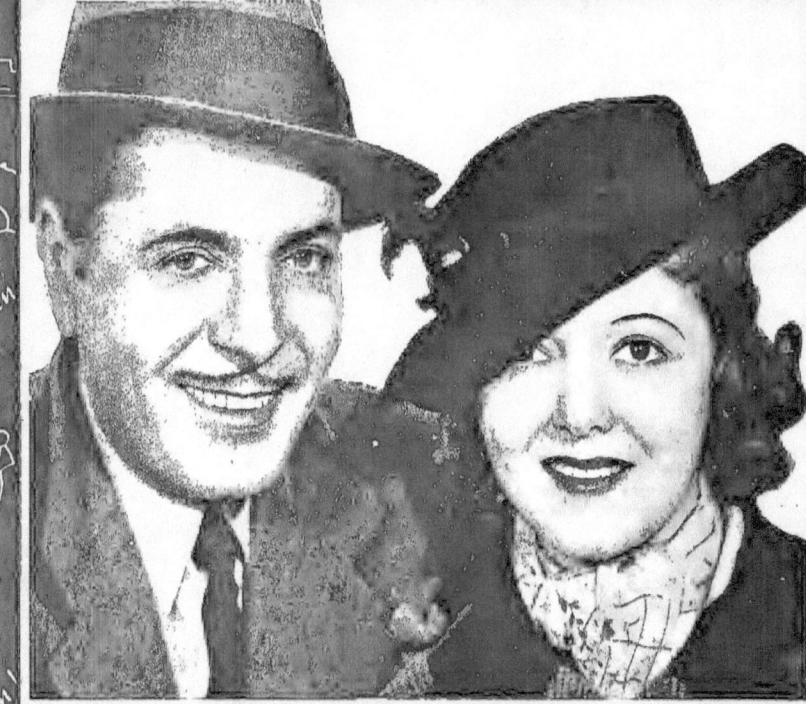

Janet **GAYNOR**
Warner **BAXTER**
in

One More Spring

with this splendid cast

WALTER KING • **JANE DARWELL** • **ROGER IMHOF**

Grant Mitchell • Rosemary Ames • John Qualen • Nick Foran

and STEPIN FETCHIT

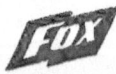

Produced by **WINFIELD SHEEHAN** • Directed by **HENRY KING**

From the Novel by Robert Nathan • Screen play and dialogue by Edwin Burke

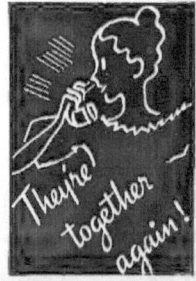

JANET'S SIDE of the Story

Has Janet Gaynor changed? Is she different off the screen? Now all the guesswork can end. She speaks out for herself—to a writer who "knew her when"!

by LLOYD BROWNFIELD

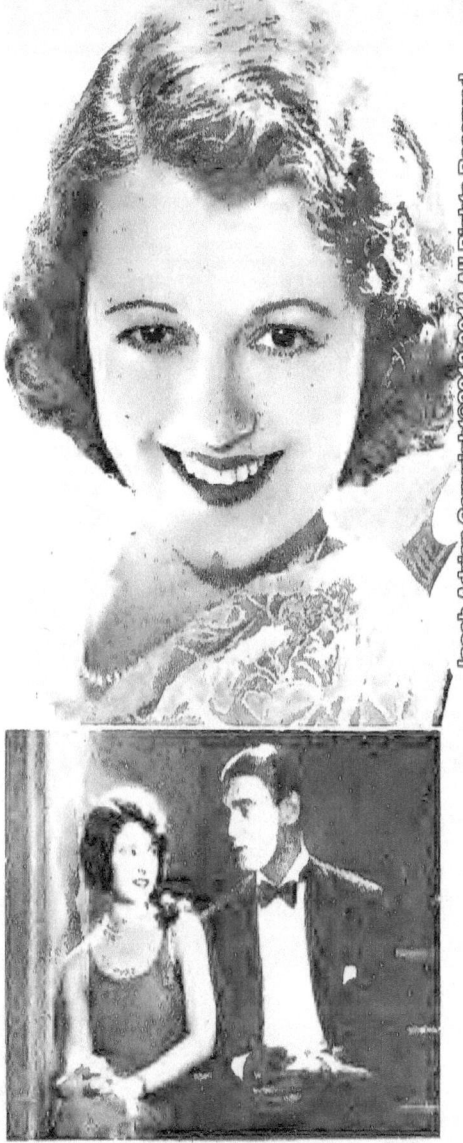

Y OU HAVE READ that Janet Gaynor has gone "difficult"—a genteel word for "high-hat"—and has no time for interviews. It is only a legend, a myth. I am a reporter, and I have just interviewed her. Rather, we have interviewed each other. For when it comes to cross-questioning, Janet can not only weather it; she can ask questions, herself.

I had unearthed what I considered one of the most valuable photographs in all Hollywood—a production "still" taken in 1925 and showing Janet Gaynor and Clark Gable seated side by side. When you stop to consider that, barring Will Rogers, Janet and Clark are the two biggest box office attractions in the film world today, you must admit that I had found a real prize. I went out to Fox Studio to try to persuade her to talk about it.

After hearing all the rumors, I was prepared for a battle to reach the Gaynor presence, as soon as I revealed that my object was an interview. No such battle was necessary. I stated my mission, was asked to wait, and after only a few minutes was escorted to the particular stage where Janet was working.

Curled up on a chintz-covered couch in her tiny portable dressing room on the *One More Spring* set, she greeted me with open arms and then proceeded to knock the props from under my cherished story idea. In return, however, she gave me material enough for a half-dozen yarns. . . .

● In the first place, Janet not only remembered me from the old days when she was a little "extra" girl, working for $7.50 a day (some days); she also remembered the rest of the newspaper gang with whom she had danced and partied before *Seventh Heaven* rocketed her to stardom—and thousands of miles from the orbit of cub reporters and their ilk.

"Gee, Brownie," Janet laughed up at me as I stalked a bit awkwardly across her miniature boudoir, "I'm glad you came out. Where *have* you been all these years? How's your brother—and Herb—and Cub—and Milt and the rest of the bunch?"

I answered her first volley of questions and produced my precious photograph. While Janet examined this ten-year-old reminder of her "extra" days, I took stock of Janet Gaynor—1935 edition.

Who remembers when, Janet Gaynor and Clark Gable appeared together for $7.50 a day apiece? Janet, for one!

For her rôle in *One More Spring*, she was dressed in what I would classify as a "depression suit"; but (being a man) I noticed that she wore the sheerest of sheer silk stockings.

"She's prettier than ever," was my first thought. "But the little Gaynor girl I knew back in 1925 and 1926 is no more," was my second. Janet has changed amazingly—and for the better, if my opinion is worth anything.

She has the same heavy mop of coppery hair, flecked with golden high lights. She has the same warm brown eyes, the same adorable mouth, even the same tiny freckles chasing themselves across the bridge of her slightly tip-tilted nose. She's still tiny, still friendly and still charming. But she's

Janet's Side of the Story

no longer a little girl to be playfully teased. She is a beautiful young woman with a keen, flashing wit, a mind of her own, and a store of common sense in keeping with her position as one of the greatest stars the film world has known.

JANET DISMISSED MY prized picture with scant ceremony. "Of course, I remember that picture," she declared, "and I remember the Clark Gable of those days very well. Clark was just as nice then as he is now as a star. He used to have a little car and he always took a bunch of us home at the end of the day. I couldn't very well forget that!

"Clark and I worked for seven-fifty checks in that picture," Janet continued. "It was called *The Plastic Age* and was made at the old F. B. O. Studios on Gower Street. Clara Bow was the star and Gilbert Roland played one of the leading rôles. It was just about his first appearance in pictures. Donald Keith had another featured part, but Clark and I were just atmosphere."

"Were you making a pretty fair living in those days, Janet?" I asked.

"Honestly, I would have starved to death if I had depended on my 'extra' checks," she replied seriously, "and I got quite a bit of work at that. But I always had a home to go to—and I kept plugging in hopes of the chance that eventually came."

So the story about the Gable-Gaynor picture and Janet's days as an "extra" was left by the wayside and we settled down to firing questions at one another.

I wanted to find out about those reports that Janet was hard to see—that she wouldn't answer any questions until she had carefully considered each one—and that several magazine writers had aroused her ire during the past few months. So

I cautiously steered the conversation around to the subject of interviews and interviewers.

To my surprise, she talked freely. I've questioned killers, bandits, burglars and high-binders of all kinds in my day as a police reporter and I'm not exactly bashful when it comes to rapid-fire cross-examination. But Janet never flinched. She answered every question.

"WRITE WHAT YOU really think," Janet told me when I asked her if there were any strings to the interview. "I'm not afraid of honest opinions, but it does irritate me when writers say things that, down in their own hearts, they don't believe, themselves.

"I object to a certain type of magazine story," Janet declared, "because of the carefully-handled innuendo which leaves the impression with readers that I'm two-faced—the impression that, although I may play nice-girl parts on the screen, I'm not necessarily the same kind of girl in private life.

"The writers, themselves, know they're unfair," continued the now thoroughly aroused little redhead, "for if they know me at all, they should know that I live a perfectly sane and normal life away from the studio.

"I don't mind it when they write that I've grown up. Of course, I'm grown up. Anyone who saw *Seventh Heaven* should understand that I *must* be grown up by this time. But I really make an honest effort at sincerity—both on the screen and off—and if my efforts are not entirely successful, it's not because I don't try."

If more proof was needed, I got it within the next few minutes. Janet was called on the set and I slipped out to watch her go through a scene with Warner Baxter and Walter King. There was no "com-

plete transformation" when she stepped under the lights. The Janet I had been talking to was the same Janet who played the scene. Her voice probably lacked the indignation aroused by some of my questions, but it was the same voice—the same girl.

When Janet returned, I asked her about her recent European trip, about her "holiday home" in Hawaii and about the fun she had enjoyed in a camp in northern Wisconsin.

"I'VE LEARNED," SHE pointed out, "that it doesn't pay to travel 'grand.' You can have a lot more fun just running around with a bunch of good friends and avoiding the pomp and ceremony of the big hotels and liners.

"Over in Europe this last time, we rented a little car and drove down through Southern France. There were several friends in the group and my mother was along. No one paid the slightest bit of attention to us and, gee, we had a good time!

"Even in Honolulu," Janet declared, "the folks who spend a lot of money and try to buy their good times usually leave feeling cheated, while I can have the time of my life just playing around our little place and making friends with the natives and the regular residents."

A chance question revealed that I had spent the Summer of 1932 in the South Seas and Janet, figuratively speaking, leaped on me with both feet.

"Oh, I'm just dying to go there. How did you like it? How long does it take? What sort of hotels are there and are the native girls pretty?"

She fired questions so fast that I had to call a halt and explain that, officially at least, *I* was the interviewer and *she* the interviewee.

I warned her not to expect romance in Tahiti—but to take her romance along. Janet grinned and nodded, admitting that she had figured on the same problem. For the first time she evaded one of my direct questions—she wouldn't reveal whether or not she had anyone in mind for the trip.

"BUT WHY IS it, Brownie," was Janet's next question, "that you go to Tahiti and have a marvelous time, and other friends of mine have made the trip and figured it just so much wasted time?"

I pointed out that she had answered that question, herself. Folks who go down in style—and live in a grand manner—always miss about nine-tenths the fun. While other visitors hired hula dancers to appear before them—I went out on the native parties and danced the hula right along with 'em.

"Of course," agreed Janet, "that's probably just as true in Tahiti as it is in Hawaii, or in Europe, or any other place. But are you planning to go back—"

At this moment an assistant director stuck his head in the door to notify Janet that she was wanted on the set again and I never did have a chance to answer her last question.

Having taken up some two hours of Janet Gaynor's $4,000-a-week time, I prepared to slide gracefully out of the picture.

Janet gave my arm a friendly little squeeze as I left the dressing-room with the parting admonition, "I'm just crazy to ask more questions about the South Seas. Come out again soon. And let's get the old gang together once more. I'll call you up the first free evening I have."

Between you and me and that gate post over there—I wonder if she ever will?

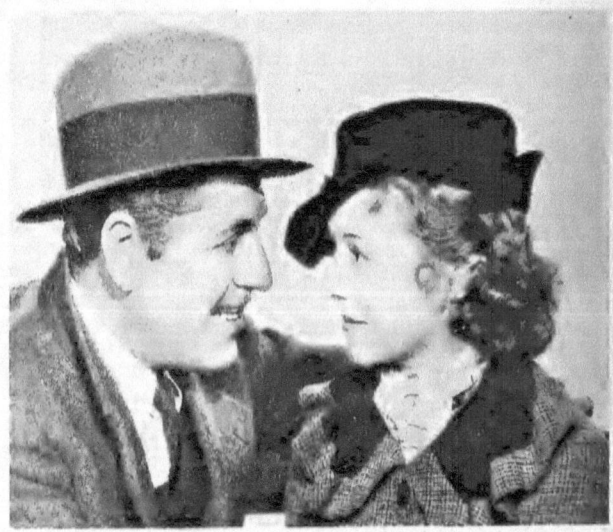

In this particular scene from One More Spring, *Janet seems to be paying rapt attention to Warner Baxter's side of the story. And what is the story? A light-hearted fantasy of a depression winter—with both in unexpected rôles*

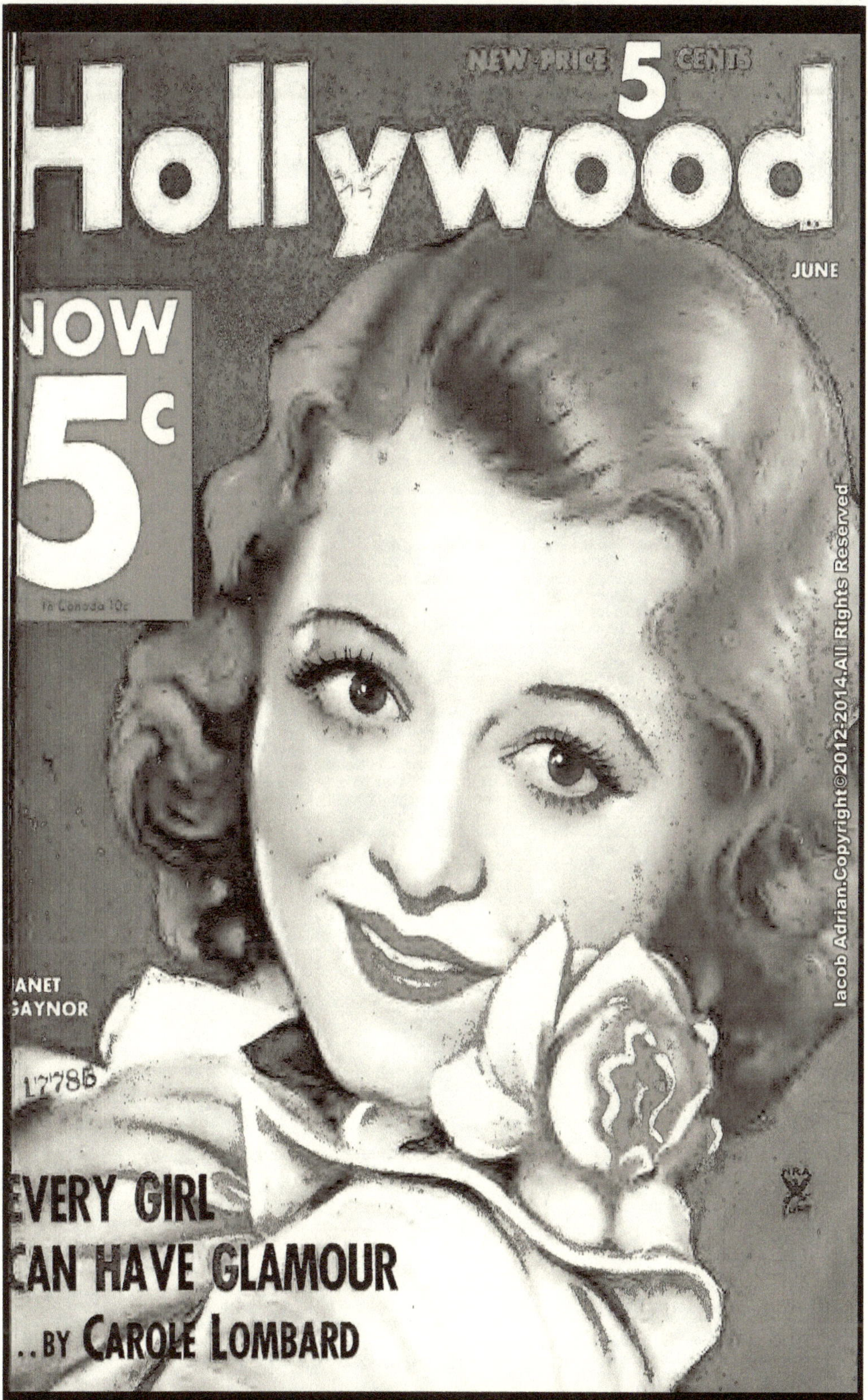

NEW PRICE **5** CENTS

Hollywood 5

JUNE

NOW 5c

In Canada 10c

JANET GAYNOR

17786

EVERY GIRL CAN HAVE GLAMOUR

...BY CAROLE LOMBARD

Solving the "Mystery" of Janet Gaynor

Janet is seldom interviewed, so it is with pride that we present this, her most revealing interview

by MARK DOWLING

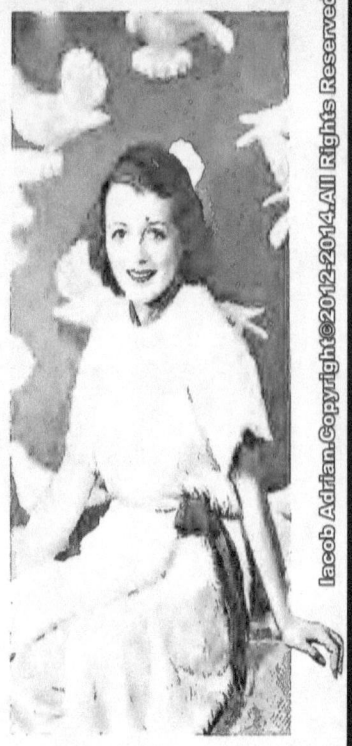

● "So Far as the public is concerned, I live only on the screen," said Janet Gaynor. This matter-of-fact statement by the star who has been voted Public Favorite Number One started many rumors that the little Gaynor is "going Garbo"—that she has become the least-known star in the movie colony. Editorials have tried to define her appeal and writers have sought reasons for her silence.

Janet explains: "My fan mail tells me that people in all parts of the world believe the shadow self of me they see on the screen is real. Why, as far back as when we made *Street Angel*, and I wore clothes that were little better than rags, I received letters even from foreign countries such as Italy offering to send me dresses, shoes, and stockings to replace those I wore in the picture. They thought those rags were all I could afford, and through pity and kindness wanted me better clothed.

"To me, *that is romance*. It is my real self masquerading as romance. What could be more romantic than when a character one plays on the screen is so realistic that the people who pay to get into the theater come to believe her an actual living person?

"That's what every player strives for —to create a perfect illusion in each rôle—to make a living, breathing person on the screen. I have been fortunate. My parts have always been romantic. Most are of the Cinderella motif. And who can challenge the romance of the most celebrated figure of fiction and fairy tale?

"*I believe in keeping illusion intact!*"

Meanwhile, with a customary delight in dramatic legend, Hollywood has p i c t u r e d Janet Gaynor as a princess locked in a tower—yearning to speak but forbidden by stern decrees of her studio bosses. You have read stories of her longing to break through the walls of silence and to open her heart to interviewers. They're decidedly not true!

"What do we go to the theater for?" Janet asks intelligently. "To be entertained—to lose ourselves in the story

being lived before our eyes, forget our troubles, and relax. Why should anyone take a little pleasure away from that entertainment by showing the public 'how the wheels go round'?

"If people like to think of me and believe in me as the person I portray on the screen, why should they be disillusioned by having my off-screen personality thrust upon them? *I believe the curtain should be drawn on the personal lives of screen players, and the romance of their screen characters kept alive!*"

And in a town where celebrities frequently bewail—sincerely or otherwise —the publicity given their "private" lives, Janet alone has achieved real privacy with quiet good taste and a complete absence of fireworks.

Not a dozen of her fellow stars even know where she lives. And where speculation about Garbo used to be Hollywood's favorite indoor sport, now you'll find the other stars discussing Janet, all the way from heated arguments as to how she has remained so securely at the top of the box-office list to her rumored romances.

● EVEN THOUGH she makes no attempt at disguise, she is seldom recognized even when she goes shopping in Hollywood. Wearing simple clothes and going about her few errands in a quite straight-forward, business-like fashion, she passes for an ordinary American girl instead of a movie star— and delights in her obscurity.

After a trip to Europe, she confided, happily to a friend, "Only one person recognized me on the whole trip—an

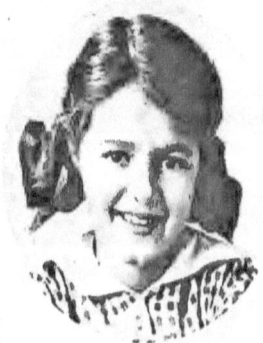

A hitherto unpublished picture of Janet at the age of eight when she attended school in Philadelphia, her native city

No need for her sympathetic fans to offer to send Janet clothes. Although she may wear rags on the screen, her personal wardrobe is smart and chic. Witness this new white fur negligee

American sailor who saw me hunting through bookstalls along the Quais in Paris. He cried, 'Gee, it's good to see an American girl over here!' and followed mother and me around all the rest of the afternoon."

It's hard to imagine such an incident happening to one of the flashy, glamourous stars—and this may explain why little Gaynor is the best beloved.

● "PLEASE DON'T quote me too often," she begs smilingly after an interview. "Just because people like to see me on the screen doesn't mean they're interested in my personal opinions. I feel so *silly* when I go into a hairdresser's and see someone reading an interview I've given. The thought that anyone might think I'm anxious to put myself on record as believing this or that is actually embarrassing. Reporters fill column after column with quotations from movie stars on all conceivable subjects, and my reaction to it all is—*who cares?*"

But she makes no frantic attempt to dodge newshawks, as Garbo and Hepburn have done. When an occasional writer is admitted to her set, she receives him with a firm handshake and chats

Mystery of Gaynor

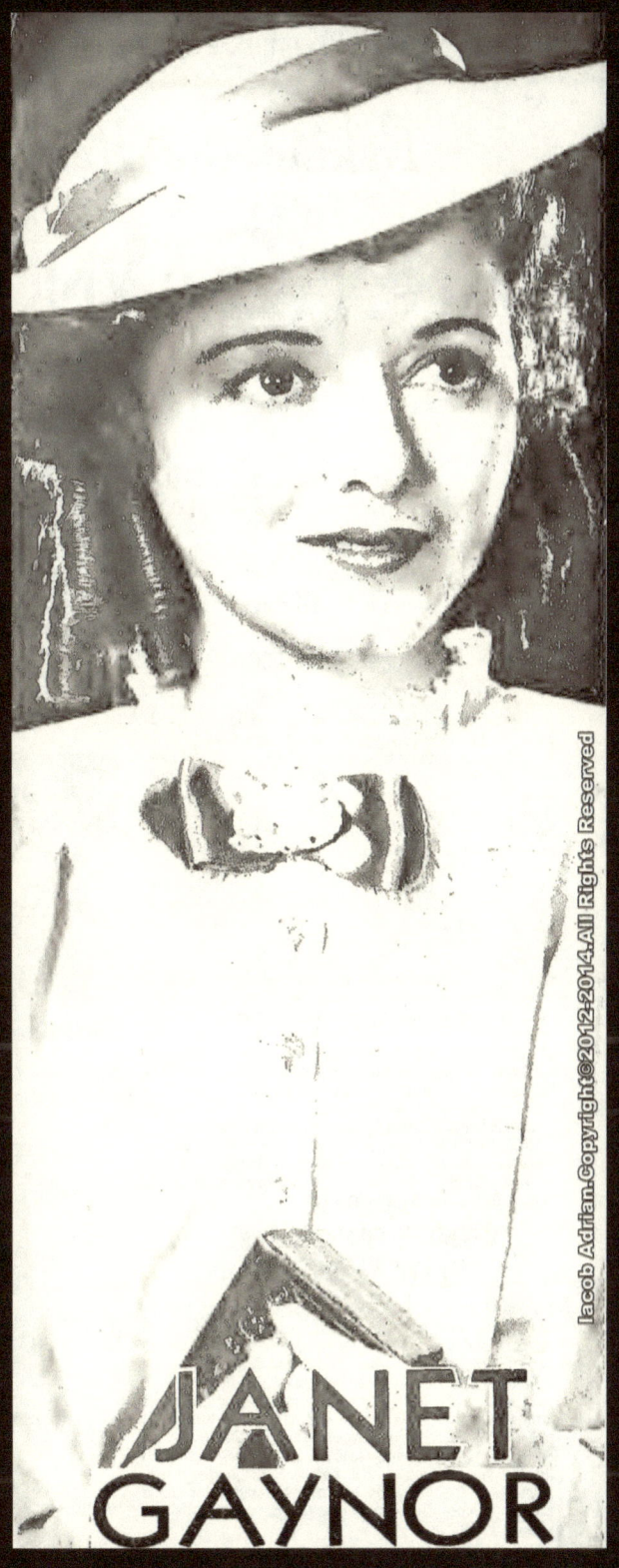

frankly over a wide range of topics.

She told me, "I certainly haven't *tried* to be a hermit! There was a story that I used the name of Mary Smith on one of my vacations to avoid being recognized, but it wasn't true. My interests just don't lie along spectacular lines, and I live so simply that there isn't a great deal you can write about me."

For instance, she loves going to little book stores around Hollywood seeking rare editions and valuable firsts. Her tastes run all the way from philosophy to fairy tales.

Such contradictions make her all the more difficult to understand. Hollywood hasn't been able to rubber-stamp her. Producers have tried again and again to give the public "another" Gaynor by introducing shy little girls whose dress is quaintly old-fashioned and whose opinions are delivered with a pretty lisp.

Janet, herself, is a radiantly beautiful young woman with a rare sense of humor. Trips to Europe have made her a Cosmopolitan, and a keen interest in designing has given her a new chic. Once it was a studio maxim that simple afternoon frocks suited her best, with their frilly sweetness, but now she can look as ravishing in the latest from Paris.

But beneath this surface sophistication she has a fresh viewpoint that is as charming as her screen characters. Strongly optimistic, for instance, she believes that everything happens for the best—and refuses to let unpleasant things bother her.

Once when a rather cruel story about her was published, she worried for a day. Then, standing in the middle of her living-room, she said to a friend thoughtfully, "Why should I give that reporter the power to make me unhappy?" And she *made* herself stop thinking about it.

She chooses her friends and intimates from charming and interesting people who have travelled and know the byways and highways of the world. Aside from her screen creations, she does other types of creative work, sketches and paints.

Each new picture is an adventure to her, and this helps to explain her amazing hold on the public. For seven years she has been one of the most popular stars in Hollywood, despite tremendous competition and changing tastes in entertainment. And this terrific popularity can be largely credited to her own efforts and keen perception. Glamour queens, "sexy" stars, and others have come and gone, but Janet still triumphantly tops the list.

"Romance will always be the most popular theme in motion pictures," she observes shrewdly. "There are success stories, mystery stories, comedy and adventure, but a cynic might say that we like romance best because for every ten people who achieve success or who find adventure or mystery in their lives, *only one finds real romance*."

In her own life, romance is the breath of life to her, and many of her best friends believe that it has recently come to her.

Mimicry, surprisingly enough, is one of her least-known talents, but when she does a "take-off" on someone she has seen on the screen, she can hold a roomful of friends spellbound and delighted.

But this and other details of her private life she prefers to keep private, with a matter-of-fact intelligence which Hollywood has somewhat underestimated.

JANET GAYNOR

Behind the Headlines in

JANET GAYNOR'S LIFE

Photos by *Charles Rhodes,*
HOLLYWOOD's *Candid Cameraman*

A Hollywood newspaper reporter gives you this intimate glimpse of the stories behind the news

by MURIEL BABCOCK

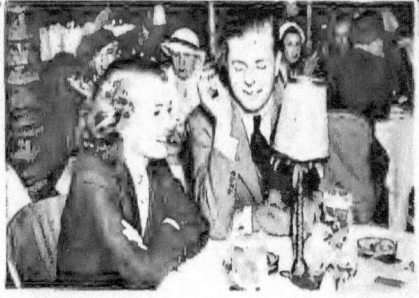

Oft-mentioned in print as "a San Francisco Doctor," it was not until recently that our cameraman snapped Dr. Veblen, the favored Gaynor companion, dining with Janet

FOR TEN YEARS, Janet Gaynor has been crashing the headlines of daily newspapers printed the world over. Since 1925 when she first landed on the drama page of a metropolitan paper, stories galore have been printed about Janet, about her love affairs, about her rôles in pictures, about her marriage and its unsuccessful culmination, about her private life, her friendships, her home at the beach, her luxurious, roomy mansion in the heart of Hollywood.

Newspaper headlines and newspaper yarns tell only half the real truth. There's always a story behind the story which cannot be revealed until later. It's the interesting but unprinted grist known only to those "in the know" in Hollywood which comprises the real story.

You know of Janet Gaynor's career in pictures. You must know that this sweet, winsome heroine of so many storybook films from Fox studio has developed, in ten years, into a woman of character and tastes far apart from the bright-eyed little girl you still see flashing across the screen. The cute, perky, red-headed little feminist of determination and will, who crashed Hollywood when still in her teens has enjoyed a romantic, glamorous career, to be sure. She has also known great heartbreak. She has had to fight to sustain her position as Ingenue No. 1 of Hollywood.

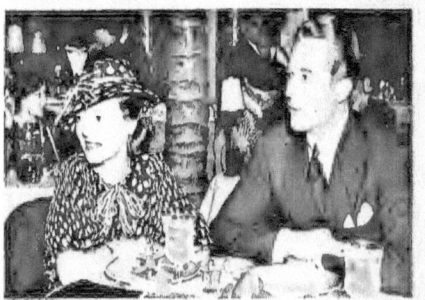

Outings with Gene Raymond have no romantic inference, although gossip columns often mention their appearance at night spots of Hollywood, claiming this to be a love affair

Here, for the first time, is the story behind the headlines—the authentic headline history of Janet Gaynor. It begins on April 25, 1925, when was printed under a two-column banner in the Los Angeles Times:

"UNKNOWN FILM ASPIRANT INTERVIEWS BIG DIRECTOR"

Janet Gaynor, a little, unknown screen aspirant, yesterday had an interview with Edwin Carewe, ace Hollywood director, and asked advice on how to proceed on screen career. Mr. Carewe advised Miss Gaynor, according to the article: "Work, work, wish, and learn, and be natural in your rôles." She looked up at him gratefully and thanked him. The article ended with a comment which turned out to be prophetic, "that perhaps sometime the director would let her play the part upon which she set her heart, a worried little slavey, tormented and harassed, dirty, disheveled, downright ugly." A truly interesting ambition for she is blessed with beauty and youth, large brown eyes, curls, and dimples in her chin.

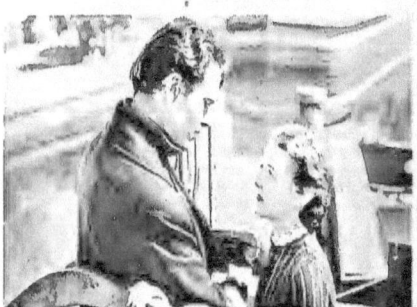

Henry Fonda, her leading man in "The Farmer Takes a Wife," was frequently mentioned in headlines as Janet's latest boy friend, but that was all publicity hooey

Flashes
your favorite stars!
by Jerry Halliday

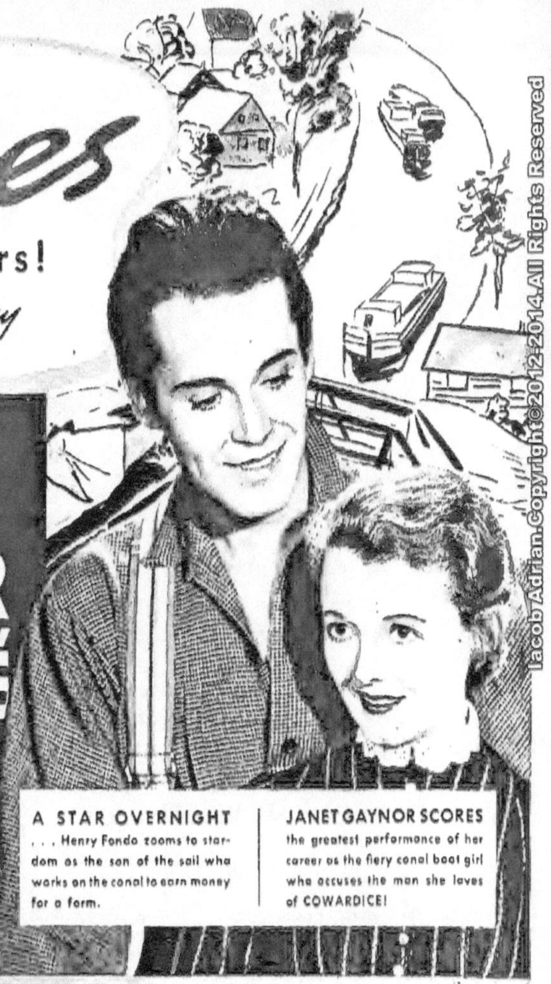

JANET GAYNOR
AND
HENRY FONDA
IN
The FARMER TAKES a WIFE

Charles Bickford   Roger Imhof
Slim Summerville   Jane Withers
Andy Devine   Margaret Hamilton

Produced by Winfield Sheehan
Directed by Victor Fleming
Screen Play by Edwin Burke
From Max Gordon's Stage Play · Authors
Frank B. Elser and Marc Connelly · Based on
the novel "Rome Haul" by Walter D. Edmonds

A STAR OVERNIGHT
. . . Henry Fonda zooms to stardom as the son of the soil who works on the canal to earn money for a farm.

JANET GAYNOR SCORES
the greatest performance of her career as the fiery canal boat girl who accuses the man she loves of COWARDICE!

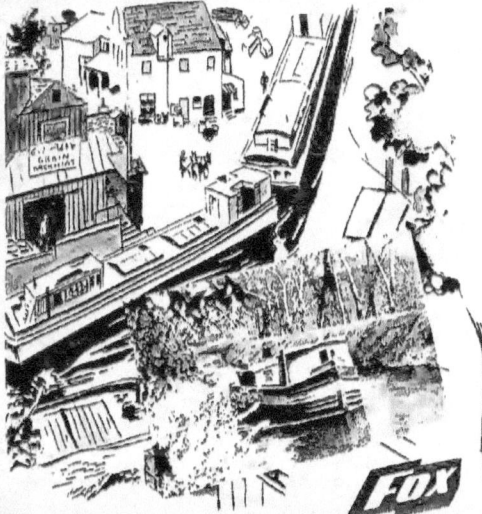

YOU . . . who loved "State Fair" . . . HAVE ANOTHER TREAT COMING!

Set in a dramatic, colorful era of American life now shown for the first time . . . when the speed of the railroad doomed the picturesque waterways . . . this story is a refreshingly new, vital, heartwarming tale of simple folk on the great Erie Canal, when it was one of the world's wonders, the gateway through which civilization took its Westward march . . . when its lazy waters rang with the shouts of swaggering boatmen, bullying their women, brawling with their rivals.

Through it all threads the romance of a kissable little miss who hides her sentimental yearnings behind a fiery temper . . . while a dreamy lad, homesick for the soil, contends for her affection with the mighty-fisted bully of the waterways.

Ask your theatre manager when he plans to play it!

FOX

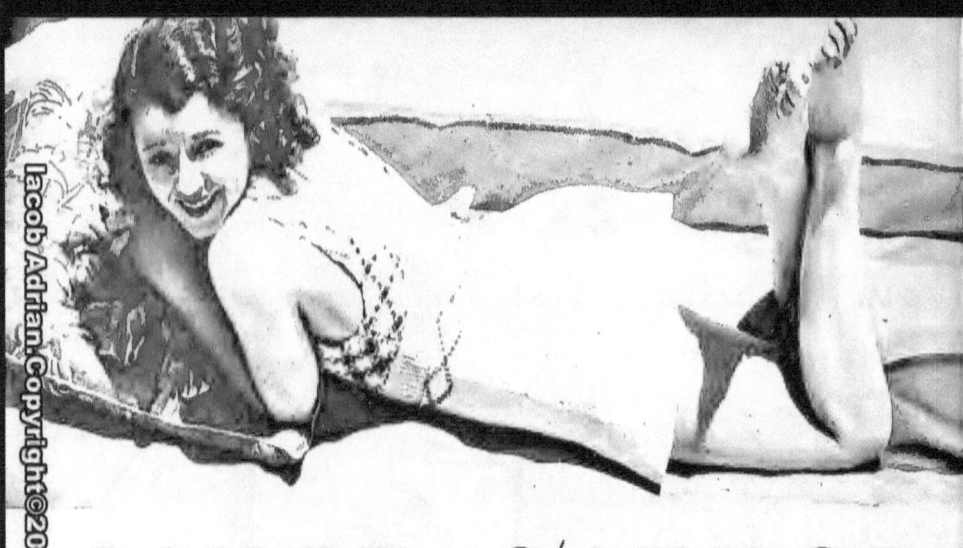

JANET GAYNOR
answers her fans

The 11,000 letters a month that come her way positively thrill Janet Gaynor! It's a big task to read them, but she loves it!

by CARL VONNELL

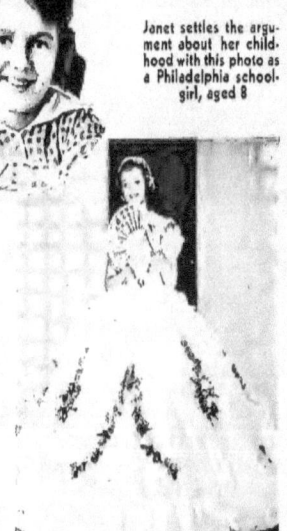

Janet settles the argument about her childhood with this photo as a Philadelphia school-girl, aged 8

Janet sent a pattern of this dress to a bride in Africa who wanted one exactly like it for her own wedding gown

THERE'S A BURLY British trooper far off in Pashawa, India, who calls himself "the baby soldier" because he bawls every time he sees Janet Gaynor weeping on the screen. . . .

Ten thousand miles away, in Stockton, California, there's a little girl whose grandmothers are peeved because she was named "Janet" instead of after either of THEM. . . .

The Command Story

You asked for Janet this month, now mail us your next request

Across the continent, off Wilmington, Delaware, a satisfied fisherman rides a home-built boat name "Tess" and in her cabin hangs an autographed photo of Janet as "Tess of the Storm Country.". . .

Down in Durban, on Africa's southern tip, is a bride whose wedding-gown was the exact replica of the crinoline Janet wore in *Carolina*, remember? . . .

In Cambridge, Massachusetts, scores of serving girls and maids all wear uniform caps exactly like the one Janet wore in *Servant's Entrance*—they made 'em themselves. . . .

Janet Gaynor herself knows all these facts.

What's more, she knows thousands of other intimate, personal facts about thousands of people all over the world—north, east, south, west. She knows them not because she's a sort of Miss Believe-It-Or-Not-Ripley, but because the people themselves tell her so.

In short, she knows because she's the living refutation of the canard that "film stars don't read their fan mail."

● JANET DOES READ hers. I know—because I caught her at it. And found her

Janet Gaynor Answers Her Fans

completely surrounded by stacks of letters, from so far-flung places that the very stamps on them made my stamp-collector's soul jitter with covetousness!

CONWAY, ARK., was the postmark on one letter.

"The Children's Literary Class of Arkansas State Teachers College," it read, "is making a study of the favorite children's books of well known people * * * would like to know what your favorite book was when you were a child * * * and why * * *"

There was a far-far-away look in Janet's eyes as I looked up. I had to ahem at her to bring her back. "Sorry," she said, "I was back in my kid days. It was Hans Christian Andersen's Faery Tales that was my favorite book then."

"Why?" I asked, reading the letter, which was written by one of the students.

"Why?—why, because Hans' faeries and shining princes and terrifying witches and awesome giants and brave Jacks and palaces and magic and romance—because those factors took me away from Everyday Land into Make-believe Land. I never got over loving to live in Make-Believe Land—that's why I'm happy today, doing what I am. Not just living there in my work, but taking thousands of other people there with me, away from the humdrum of today into the escape and romance and happiness of Make-Believe Land . . ."

She giggled. I wanted to know what was funny about that.

"Well—I've a confession," she grinned like an imp. She pointed to a bookshelf. There stood one of those big-typed kids' editions of Faery Tales. "I still read 'em," she said, and dove into another letter, which came from Asheville, North Carolina.

"* * * ask if you would send me the recipe for some little dish we could serve at our club to add a little personal touch to our meetings, where we can discuss you as though you were with us."

"H'm—now what shall—oh, I have the VERY thing!"—and Janet hooved from the big chair, scattering letters like a cyclone, and into the kitchen. I picked up one with a 2-anna-6-pies stamp of India on it. It turned out to be from British Tommy in Pashawa. There were four closely written pages of adulation. "I'm not asking for correspondence, though—because my little Pal would not like it * * * please think of me as 'the baby soldier' who goes to see you on the screen * * * and YOU are the one who can bring tears to a soldier's eyes * * *"

● JANET WAS back, with a recipe card. She pinned it to the letter from North Carolina. "I'll send her my Ice-Box Cookies recipe; gosh, how I LOVE 'EM," she explained. She showed me the card—

1 pound butter
1½ cups sugar
Dates and nuts to suit
5 cups flour
3 eggs
Vanilla flavoring

Cream the butter and sugar; add the eggs one by one, beating and mixing meanwhile; add the five cups of flour gradually while beating the mixture; add the dates and nuts which have been pre-

viously chopped fine; add the flavoring. Shape this into a roll; put in the ice-box over night; in the morning, slice into thin layers—making the cookies—and bake in a moderate oven.

While I was copying the recipe for you, Janet was laughing over what looked like an overgrown Chinese laundry ticket. It was a letter, from China, and attached to it, a translation from the Fox studio's interpreting office. You can't translate Chinese word-for-word, but the letter came from a wealthy Chinaman who explained that he and an English official had seen Delicious when it showed in Shanghai. Sure of his knowledge, the Englishman had said the musical bottle had played a certain old English folksong. Educated in England, the Chinese insisted it was another tune. They made a bet.

"My Chinese friend was right," said Janet. "The tune the bottle played was 'Somebody From Somewhere.' I'll write and tell him so—and make the Englishman pay up!"

● THE NEXT letter was to settle another argument: A San Francisco woman and some relatives of hers in Philadelphia, were burning up the mails. The former insisted Janet was a "San Francisco girl, born and educated in San Francisco, ushered in a local theater, graduate of Polytechnic High School. My Philadelphia relatives are positive you are a product of that city. I'd like to mail your reply to them and show them!"

Both Janet's hands went high in the air. "Isn't that what a prize-fight referee does when it's a draw?" she asked. "I'm going to tell her that I was born in Philadelphia, started my education there; then moved later to San Francisco where, as she says, I DID usher in a movie house and graduate from Poly Hi. And I call BOTH cities 'home.' Look, I've even got some pictures of myself taken when I was a schoolgirl in Philadelphia."

She showed them to me. I'm showing one of them to you, herewith. For a couple of hours, then, we went through the mail—the letter from a "group of girls doing household employment in Cambridge, Mass., who asked Janet how to make the cap she wore in Servant's Entrance because "we're all crazy about the cap and are dying to make ourselves one like it." Janet was going to have the studio wardrobe department send them a model.

● FROM A GIRL in Claremont, The Mall, Brading, Isle of Wight, England, came "a little love story written by my mother ten years ago," and which she thought Janet might like to put on the screen. "I get lots like this, but I have to turn them all over to the studio story department at once," Janet explained.

There was a whole stack of letters, asking Janet to send the writers the clothes she no longer wanted. "If I send each one even a tiny thing," she said, face serious, "I'd have to be the Dionne quintuplets hundreds of times over. As a matter of fact, all my clothes, when I no longer wear them, go to a little friend who needs them."

The hundreds of letters asking for autographs and signed pictures were in another pile. You see, Janet gets so many thousands of fan letters that they are

opened and segregated for her—but eventually, Janet reads them herself. "Why," she explains, "when people think enough of me to go to the bother of writing, pouring out their hearts and souls to me, addressing them, putting a stamp on them, mailing them—why then the least I can do for these grand friends is to read what they say, and answer them when an answer is called for, don't you think?"

"Not all screen stars feel that way," I reminded her.

"But I do," she said simply. "Except—" (and now she has on that imp-grin of hers again) "—except the chain letters! I got 450 of them in a single day!"

● A LETTER from a man in Bombay contended, in 14 typed pages, that movie theaters should spray scents and odors through the house in keeping with the scene on the screen. A couple in Honolulu wanted her to indorse a song they had written. A woman in Roumania sent a package which contained a hand embroidered tea spread and napkins. She showed me the letter from the South Africa girl, to whom she'd sent a pattern of the crinoline from Carolina to be worn as a wedding gown. There were scores of letters asking how tall she was, how much she weighed, whether she liked tennis, coffee, blue, jazz music, perfume, skating, eggs, travel and a million other things. Each letter was to be answered.

I looked up from a letter of an 87-year old Iowa farmer who was making up a Janet Gaynor scrapbook, believe it or not, to see Janet with eyes bright with tears.

There were two letters in her hand—one from the St. Louis Children's Hospital. "I am a girl of thirteen years of age. You have always been my favorite movie actress. The last picture I saw you in was Daddy Long Legs, for I have been in the hospital for nearly two years. I wanted so much to see you in One More Spring but the nurses who have seen it told me all about it, which is next best. I am making a scrapbook of nothing but pictures of you and wondered if you would send me an autographed picture of yourself for the front of the book . . ."

● THE OTHER, in the bold handwriting of a society girl was in the same envelope:

"My Dear Miss Gaynor—

For my Junior League work I have been visiting this child for the past two years, reading to her, or bringing her a little cheer in her lonely cot in the Children's Hospital.

She is paralyzed from her waist down, and will probably never walk again. She lives in hopes of seeing you in a moving picture again, but probably never will.

So if you want to add a big thrill to her lonely existence, you will give her letter your personal attention, for she will be waiting anxiously for a picture. I believe you have a heart and will do this!"

Janet's eyes brimmed over. Heart?—may I tell the society girl in St. Louis that if she'd been there with Janet that moment, she'd have known darned well that the smiling redhead has a heart as big as St. Louis! Janet was already reaching for paper and pen . . .

"Poor, dear kid—I wish—I wish I were one of Hans Andersen's faery queens," she whispered, "so I could touch her poor little legs with my magic wand—and make her walk again . . ."

Janet Gaynor's Lucky Accident

WHEN JANET GAYNOR collided with Henry Fonda and suffered a concussion which forced her to withdraw from the cast of *Way Down East*, she thought that her luck had treated her most shabbily.

Actually it was a lucky accident. Janet escaped from an assignment which turned out badly, and she won a rest at a time when it was most needed.

Never strong, her program at the old Fox lot called for a constant succession of pictures, all of them sapping her small strength. Being a top notch star, there was no rest for Janet Gaynor. That stumble and fall was nothing short of providential. The result: A long rest, with complete recovery; a chance to survey her work and gain a new perspective; a new role in what promises to be one of the best pictures in her career.

That is why Janet is spotlighted this month in HOLLYWOOD. As usual, Janet emerges from a bout with adversity, to show Hollywood that nothing can down her. The title of one of her early pictures has always been prophetic of the Gaynor career; it was called *Lucky Star*. She was undoubtedly born under one, on that sixth of October, 1907.

A dicker with M-G-M took her away, on loan, from her home studio, the new 20th Century-Fox company headed by

another lucky and clever person named Darryl Zanuck, to star in *Small Town Girl*.

● WHAT STAR COULD ask for a better break? On top of this, Metro had decided to give her Robert Taylor for a leading man. While this was going on,

Bob was over at Universal, making *Magnificent Obsession* with Irene Dunne.

Bob, needless to say, was making the most of a magnificent opportunity. The picture was an instant success. Consequently Janet had a leading man whose star was [Continued on page 65]

Janet fell on her head and was forced into temporary retirement. But she wasn't so unlucky after all, as you'll see in this story about her new picture at M-G-M

FROM STONE INTO CAT « « « GEORGIE STONE

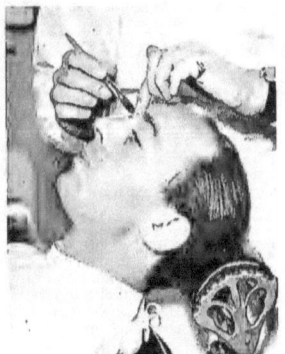

Here's Georgie Stone as you knew him in *Frisco Kid*. The make-up artist begins work

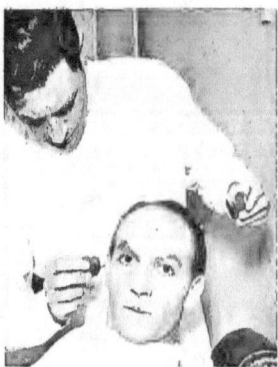

What's this! It's the half-way mark as Clay Campbell continues his alchemy of make-up

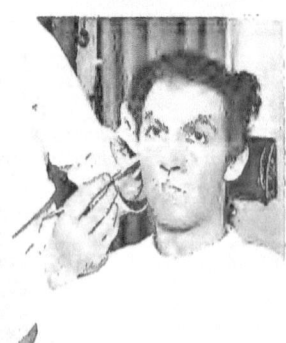

And here you have Georgie as Sanchez, the Cat, his weird rôle in *Anthony Adverse*

definitely on the ascendancy. We went to watch her make this picture, with William Wellman directing.

Janet is surprisingly small. She's only five feet tall, and seldom weighs more than 100 pounds with her pockets full. Today she was clad in a blue sailor jacket with brass buttons down the front, laced sandals which would fit a Shirley Temple doll, and a blue ribbon about her auburn hair. She has big brown eyes and a generous, mobile mouth.

Her eyes dance as she talks, her expression is constantly changing. Her small, confidential voice is the most winning part of her personality. The scene is on a boat, where she has gone with her husband, Bob Taylor.

"You see, in this picture, I've married Bob against his own wishes," Janet explains. "He didn't want a wife at all, much less me! And here I am, just a fly in the ointment. Since Bob will have nothing to do with me, I decide to enjoy myself as best I can, and so I sort of flirt with the captain to make him let me steer the boat."

● DIRECTOR WELLMAN gets the signal from his assistant that the lights are ready. He crooks a finger at Janet. The camera is trained on Ed Sullivan, the ship's captain, for this "take," and does not include Janet—that will come later. But Janet goes through the scene just as if she were in the lens, all for the benefit of big Ed Sullivan. Her face is eager, alert, filled with expression as she stands behind the camera, feeding him his lines.

"Lovely, simply lovely," grins Wellman. "Wild Bill" Wellman is another who has profited from a lucky star. He has always been a harum-scarum mugg with a genius for getting into tight spots—and out of them. Restless devils burn in his deep set eyes. During the World War he and Tommy Hitchcock, the greatest polo player in the world today, raided a German airdrome many miles inside the enemy lines. It was a mad enterprise. But it succeeded. Each time a black-crossed plane tried to get into the air after them, they'd shoot it down. The exploit was made into a film a few years back, called *The Dawn Patrol*, starring Barthelmess.

Janet likes to work with Bill Wellman. She likes a sense of humor and a daredevil disposition.

When illness forced her to weeks of quiet inactivity, she learned to take life with a grin. She had plenty of time to think. The philosophy she has evolved is simple enough—you only live once, so make each day count. She never tires of delving into new realms. She'll dive into a scientific topic and when, after wading through books and talking with well versed people on the chosen subject, she comes up for air, Janet has a pretty good notion of her topic. It is that quality of wanting to know what makes the wheels go round which has kept her in the top row of film favorites. Others may come and go, but Janet is the one unfailing star.

● ANOTHER QUALITY in her makeup is the ability to make new friends and keep old ones. Even a long vacation from the screen did not keep her off the list of topnotch stars. The following of most stars fluctuates according to their pictures. Not so with Janet. Such popularity must be deserved!

And Janet has worked hard for her place in the sun. She is the embodiment of the hope that sighs and sings in the breasts of all girls who dream of a picture career—Janet rose from the ranks as an extra girl with nothing to go on but a winning smile and ambition. Certainly Janet isn't beautiful. She proves you don't have to have the sort of face ascribed to Helen of Troy in order to succeed in pictures, and that endears her the more to girls.

She is very popular with men. Janet exerts a greater appeal than blondes with those luscious curves men are supposed to fall for. They like her sparkle, her genuineness, and her manner of friendly intimacy. Invariably one hears rumors that she is in love with her leading man. You hear that about Bob Taylor now. Well, perhaps they do fall in love with Janet, for one couldn't blame them.

● THERE ISN'T MUCH doubt that Charles Farrell fell in love with her in those glorious days when *Seventh Heaven* was the big picture of all time. Maybe Janet fell in love with him. How the public hoped they would marry! That's the sad part of Hollywood—those the fans want to see get married, seldom reach the altar with the right man. Unhappily, Janet and Charlie had one of those misunderstandings, and both promptly went out and married somebody else.

Hollywood is inclined to believe that both Janet and Charlie had a few misgivings about the end of their romance; certainly Janet's marriage to Lydell Peck didn't take. But it all matters very little now; those days are gone and forgotten, and one of these times Janet will find the man she wants, and marry him, and live happily ever after. —JACK SMALLEY

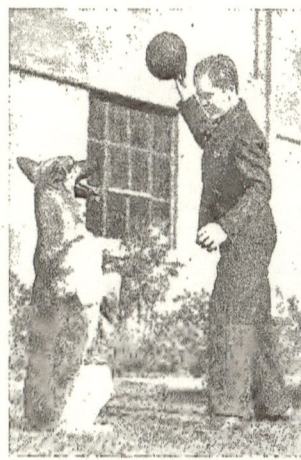

Jackie Cooper is growing up in spite of everything! He's shown here with Rin Tin Tin, Jr., his pal in M-G-M's *Tough Guy*

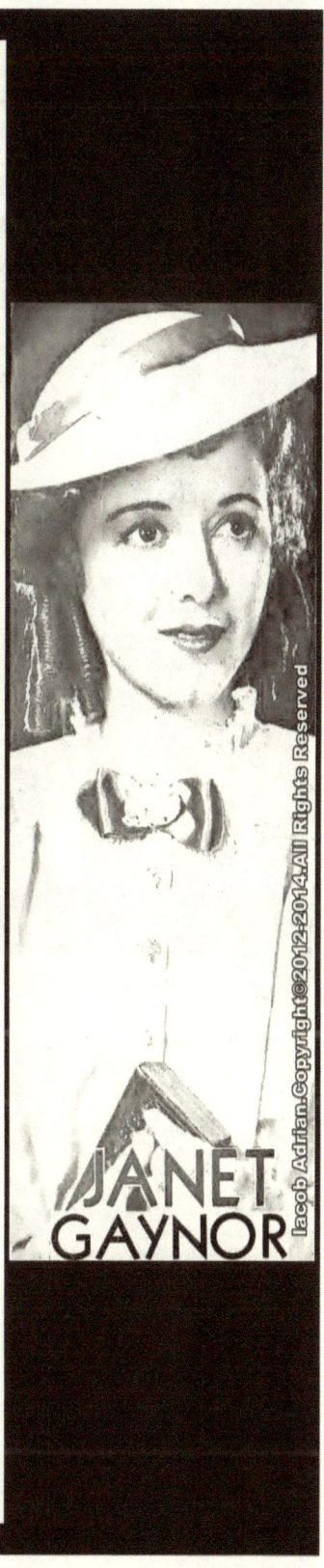

JANET GAYNOR

A Star is Born

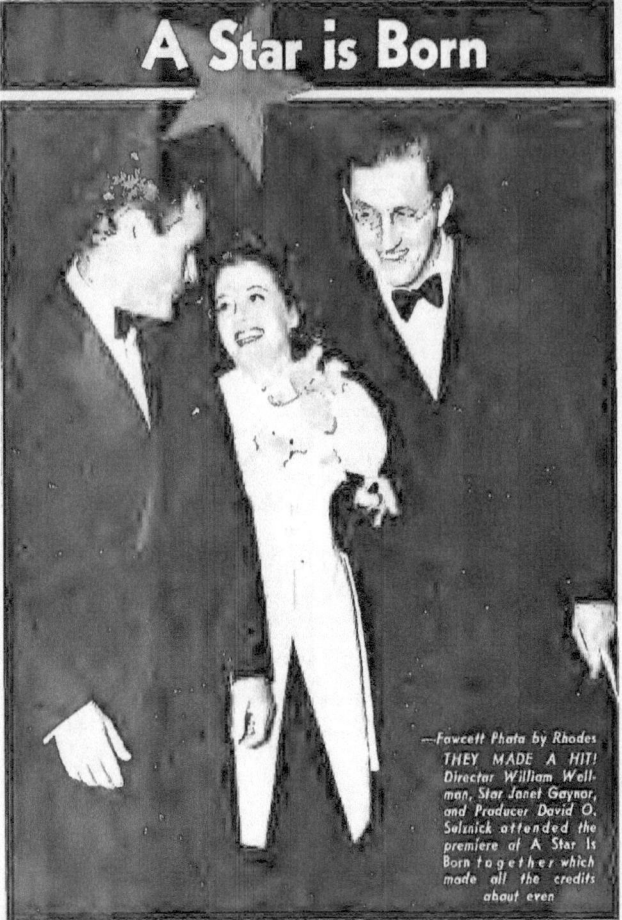

—Fawcett Photo by Rhodes
THEY MADE A HIT!
Director William Wellman, Star Janet Gaynor, and Producer David O. Selznick attended the premiere of A Star Is Born together which made all the credits about even

at the star's funeral are an exaggeration. Lionel Stander jars you just a bit with his ruthlessness at times, but all in all it's simply swell and we would be slackers not to say so. The photography is not the least of this smart picture's many attainments and if you were one who thought that Miss Gaynor was about "washed up" you've got another guess coming. A Star Is Born should make her one of the most popular stars of the year. Certainly she proves one of the most charming and competent. William Wellman becomes Woody Van Dyke's closest rival as a natural, spirited director with this film. He is entitled to far more credit than he has ever been given.

• •

NIGHT MUST FALL—(M-G-M)—Divorcing himself completely from his usual amiable and sophisticated roles,

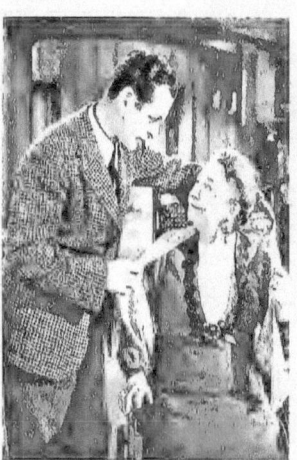

Montgomery places a shawl about the shoulders of Dame May Whitty, the woman he is about to kill in M-G-M's Night Must Fall

REVIEWS of the MONTH

HOLLYWOOD, as well as film fans all over the world, should give a great big vote of thanks to David O. Selznick for making A Star Is Born because here is perhaps the most colorful (no pun intended) and delightfully enjoyable picture with a movie background ever made. The plot amounts to little, but the picture gives a distant audience a better appraisal of the real Hollywood than anything we've ever seen. And the picture sparkles with fine performances and dialog that is brilliant because it is so natural.

A Star Is Born might also, quite fittingly, be called A Star Is Re-born, because it presents a new, winsome, lovable Janet Gaynor in a performance that surpasses the Seventh Heaven pantomime which won her her greatest previous acclaim. And, from where we were sitting it looked as if Fredric March was more natural than in any

picture since the rollicking Royal Family of Broadway.

Possibly you may have gathered the impression we liked A Star Is Born. That is hardly enough; we thought it was one whale of a picture and one that should make every person connected with this important industry proud that such entertainment can be made. The color is so perfect that you are hardly conscious of it; the actors so natural in action and coloring that you hardly realize they are, after all, but projections from tiny celluloid strips. Miss Gaynor certainly could have sold any producer the idea of making her a screen star in the screen test scene and the character Fredric March plays is that which more than one star has played in real life. Adolphe Menjou adds another splendid portrayal to his already long list and Andy Devine is splendid. Not even the ridiculous events

Robert Montgomery, as Danny, the maniacal murderer in Night Must Fall, gives a performance which, despite its macabre and sinister tone, will rank as one of the most outstanding of the year. Dominating the picture throughout its entire length, Montgomery's intensely vivid and realistic portrayal of the insane Danny will hold you spellbound from the time he appears on the screen until he makes his final exit. Night Must Fall is a horror picture, a nerve-tingling thriller the like of which has seldom been seen on celluloid—but whether you like film shockers or not, you should see the extraordinary Mr. Montgomery. Take our unbiased word for it, he gives you a genuine film treat.

Rosalind Russell, always to be counted upon for good work in any picture in

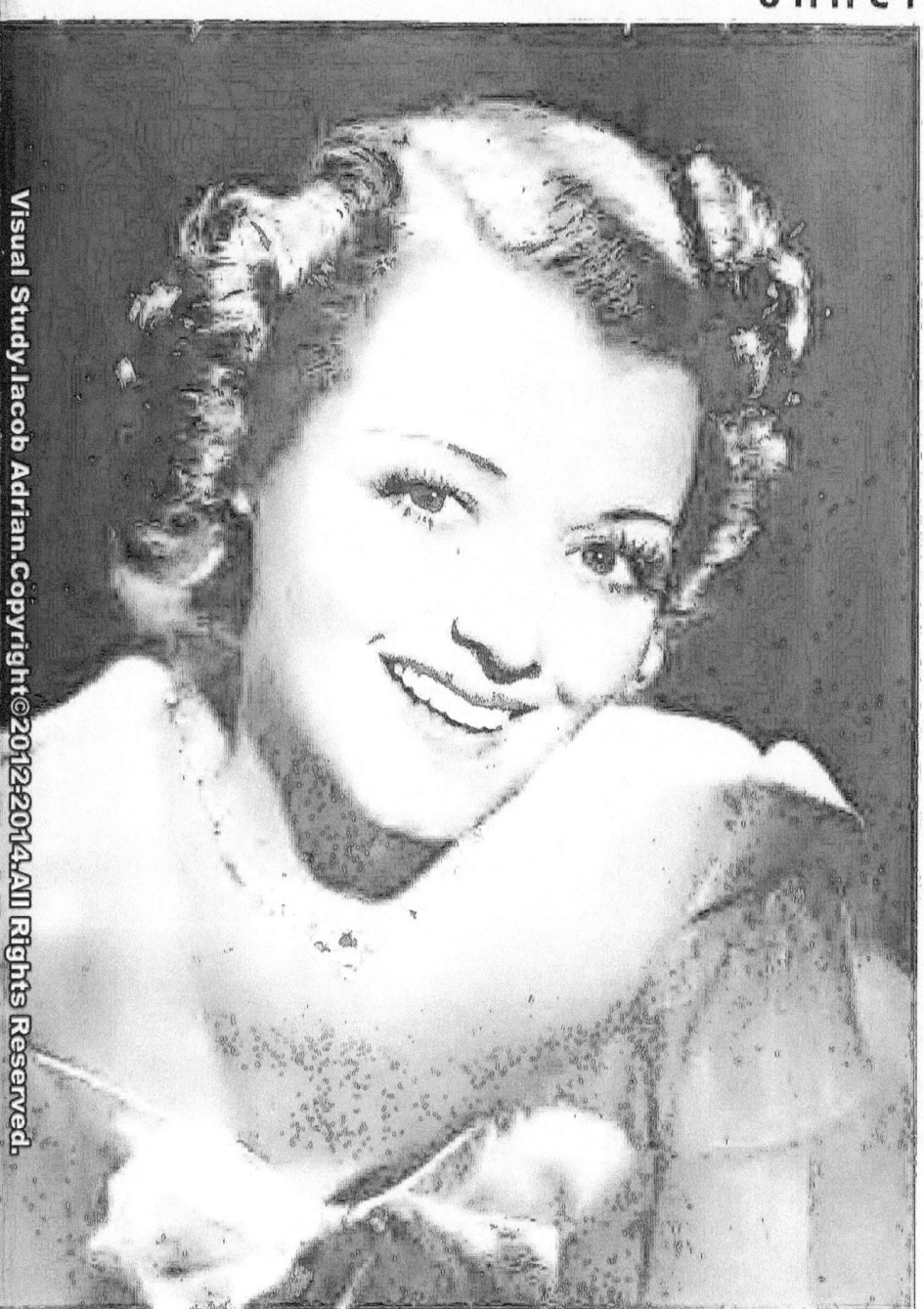

Henry Fonda's heart grew fonda on Mother's Day and among his gifts to his wife was half a horse! Both the star and his wife's rancher brother wished to buy the same animal at a Hollywood horse auction, but finally arranged a deal which satisfied all concerned. Fonda bought the horse and presented it to his wife; then gave it to her brother to have and to hold excepting at such times as his wife might be a visitor at the ranch.

The lengths to which producers of motion pictures customarily go in order to provide authentic atmosphere and backgrounds for their screenplays is aptly illustrated by *Algiers*, the Wanger opus starring Charles Boyer and Hedy (*Ecstasy*) Lamarr.

Having decided to film the picture Wanger sent detailed instructions regarding certain needed scenes to the United Artists offices in London where they were relayed to Cameraman Lloyd Knechtel. The latter journeyed to the Algerian capital on the northern coast of Africa and after obtaining the required permission from officials, shot more than 10,000 feet of the native quarter for background scenes. This footage was immediately rushed to the United Artists studios in Hollywood so that the selected bits might be incorporated in the picture. Then Knechtel returned to his base in London to await another call to some distant point in Europe, Africa or Asia.

Ed Wynn is the favorite marrying justice of the peace for filmdom's elopees.

[Continued on page 47]

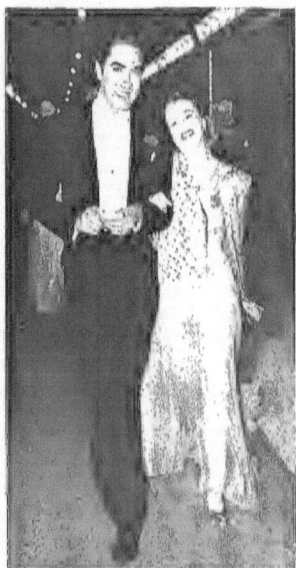

Janet Gaynor and Tyrone Power evidently found the excitement of the *Alexander's Ragtime Band* preview a lot of fun as they strode down the long runway to the theatre

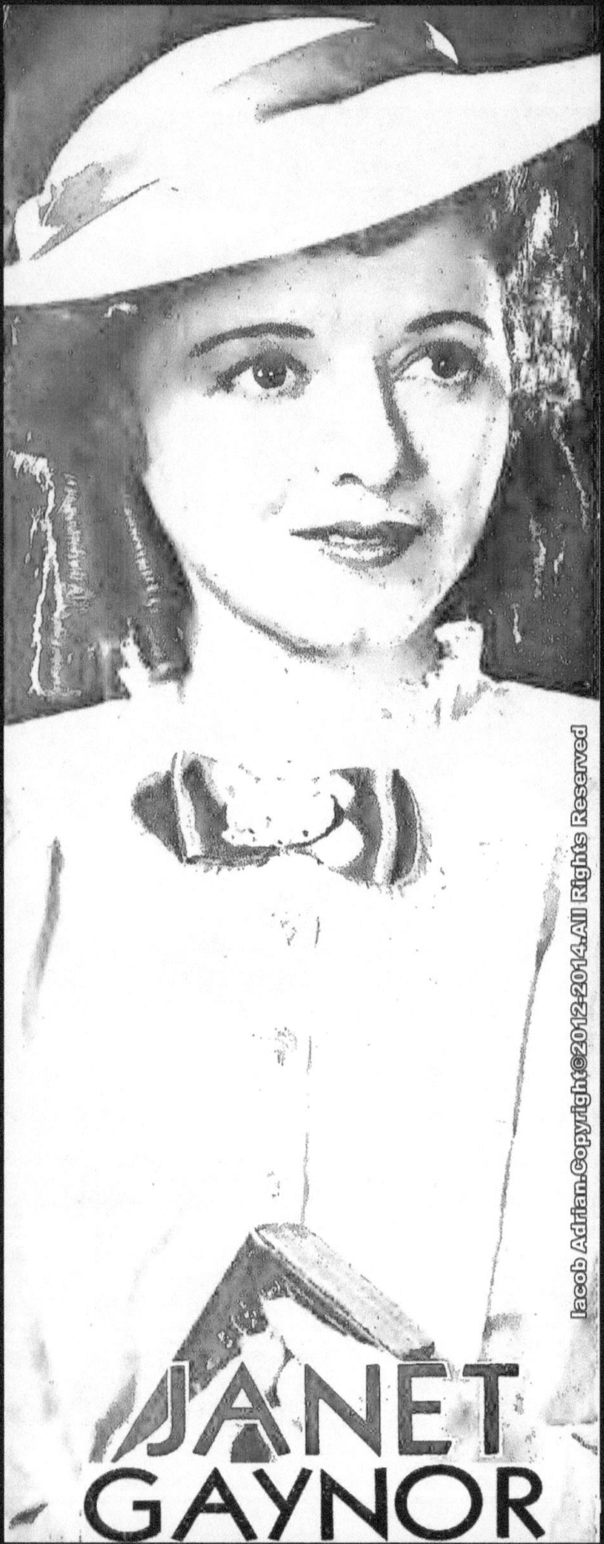

JANET GAYNOR

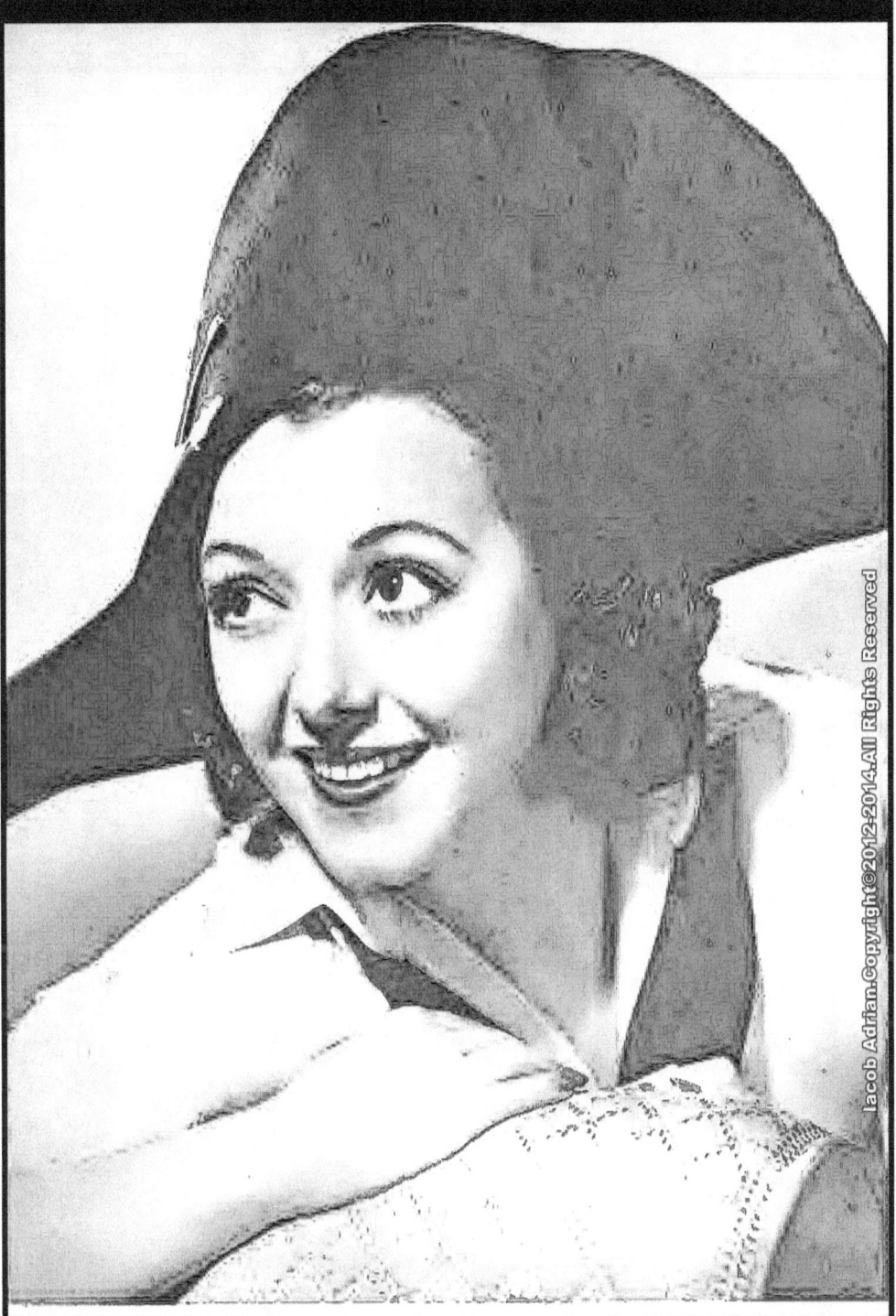

JANET GAYNOR

You'll be seeing her in two pictures this fall. One, *The Young in Heart* is the screen version of the magazine story *The Gay Banditti* which deals with the escapades of an impoverished, impractical, but delightful family. The other is *Three Loves Has Nancy*, which s o u n d s good, too

7 GREAT PERSONALITIES

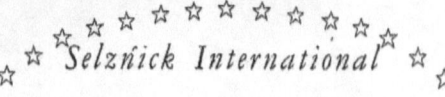

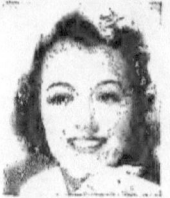

JANET GAYNOR
"A Star Is Born"

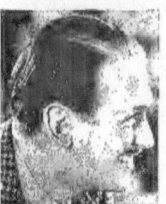

DOUGLAS FAIRBANKS, JR.
"Rupert of Hentzau"

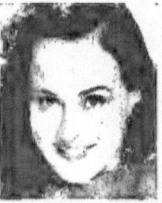

PAULETTE GODDARD
In her talking debut

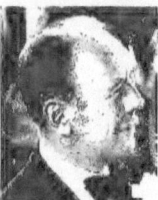

ROLAND YOUNG
First picture since "Topper"

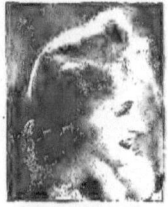

BILLIE BURKE
"Mrs. Topper"

Selznick International

presents

JANET
GAYNOR

DOUGLAS
FAIRBANKS JR.

PAULETTE
GODDARD

in

THE
YOUNG
IN
HEART

with
ROLAND YOUNG
BILLIE BURKE

with Henry Stephenson   Directed by Richard Wallace
Produced by DAVID O. SELZNICK *..Released thru United Artists*

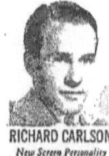

RICHARD CARLSON
New Screen Personality

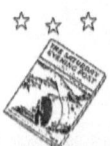

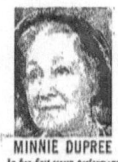

MINNIE DUPREE
In her first screen performance

From the SATURDAY EVENING POST story, "THE GAY BANDITTI," by I. A. R. Wylie

Bibliographic sources :

Hollywood (1934-1943)
Publisher: Hollywood Magazine, inc. ; Fawcett Publications, inc.

The New Movie Magazine (1929-1935)
Publisher: Tower Magazines, inc.

This documentary study use,
combined in various proportions,
elements from the following categories,
forms and subsets :
- fair use
- documentary
- documentary photography
- feature
- journalism
- arts journalism
- visual journalism
- photojournalism
- celebrity photography
in order to :
- employ material as the object of cultural critique ,
- quote to illustrate an argument or point ,
- use material in historical sequence,
providing independent opinion,
using photos, press articles, advertisements,
opinions of fans etc. ...